BATTERED, BROKEN
HEALED

Living Through Domestic Abuse

MIRIAM MWARIA

ACKNOWLEDGMENTS

To **Tracy** and **Dave Berry**, who opened up their hearts and home and resources to me when I was ready to change the direction of my life. Thank you for being true friends who leave their doors wide open for me to date. You are some of the most generous people I have ever known.

Elizabeth Wachira, my best friend, who is closer than a sister, for hanging in there with me through it all. There are no words to describe what you mean to me. I love you.

Dr. Joash and **Dr. Catherine Wambua**, for opening your hearts and home and holding my hand through the transition to the other side of this life, and for raising my son with me. Your advice and guidance have been invaluable. I am a professional today because of your guidance.

To my sister and brother-in-law **Mercy** and **Francis Mpolokoso,** for taking me in. I don't know what I would have done and where I would have gone when the time came.

To my loving, kind, wonderful husband, **Gerald Ngugi.** Thank you for loving this broken girl, and creating with me a life and home that I only dreamed of. Thank you for restoring my faith in love and marriage. Looking forward to the life that the Lord has planned for us. I love you more than I know to express.

CONTENTS

INTRODUCTION

I vividly remember a thought crossing my mind one day. I thought to myself, "One day, my heart will just quit. They will say I died of 'old age' at the age of 30." Far too many people have walked in the same shoes I have; far too many have lost the battle. Those of us who have made it through know that if left on our own we would not be where we are today. So, what is this journey I'm referring to? Domestic abuse. Domestic abuse has been defined by the National Coalition Against Domestic Violence as *the willful intimidation, physical assault, battery, sexual assault, and/or other abusive behavior as part of a systematic pattern of power and control perpetrated by one intimate*

partner against another.[1]

While there seem to be a lot of information out there, I still think that there are misconceptions or assumptions about what this entails.

I don't want to be assumptive, so I write based on my personal experience.

Have you ever had someone say something to you in anger that made you feel either defensive or made you cower away, depending on your personality? Why do we react like that? What is it inside of us that makes us respond to such treatment the way we do? I think we feel violated, misunderstood and perhaps, scared. When that happens over and over again, it is abuse. It can be physical or verbal, or emotional. Arguments are not unusual in a marriage or relationship. However, when this becomes a constant occurrence, and there is no resolution, and one person feels bullied regardless of what they do to try to keep the peace, then you better believe it, this person is being abused. Abuse is a game of control. It is not merely a one-time loss of judgment in the heat of an argument. It is calculated and habitual, almost like an art form.

An abuser can be cool as ice and make you feel like

you are the scum of the earth, all with a smile on his face. Abuse is a real problem in our society, and it does not discriminate based on race, nationality, or socio-economic status. We have a choice to make. We can address this issue or choose to ignore it. I choose to do my part by bringing to light the events of my life. My hope is that through this book I may touch one life. My prayer is that one person may choose a different path because they have read my story.

CHAPTER ONE

The Relationship

I grew up in a loving Christian home as the middle child in a family of five siblings. I had a normal childhood characterized by the usual sibling rivalry, childhood games, school, and homework. I grew up in Kenya, East Africa. I was a typical good Christian girl who never got into any kind of serious trouble. In fact, I was really quite responsible by the time I got into high school and was a leader in various capacities. A couple of years after high school, I got the opportunity to move from my home country to attend college. It was here that I met the man who would eventually become my husband. It was during our first week of freshman orientation. My roommates and I met a group of guys who lived in the school apartments that were available for those not on a full boarding scheme. As the weeks went on, we struck a friendship with the guys and started socializing. I remember how he took a quick interest in me. His blue eyes intrigued me. The diamond stud he wore in one ear stirred my curiosity. Gradually, we began to have conversations, take walks together and spend a lot of our free time together. He started writing me beautiful poetry. I never had so much attention from a man before. I was always focused and didn't really take any of the boys who were interested in me seriously. Up until this time, I had one major crush after high school—my childhood friend. However, we just remained friends. Now, for the first time, I had someone interested in me who pursued me relentlessly, and really seemed to love me.

I remember our first Valentine's Day. It was like something out of a fairytale. He sent me on a scavenger hunt around campus. Each stop had a note and a flower, pledging his love. The scavenger hunt eventually led to where he was, and he took me out to eat at one of our favorite restaurants. It was great. He was charming, and we enjoyed each other's company. However, a few subtle signs started to emerge. He seemed to get into trouble quite often. Some of my friends started to caution me about him. They saw a side of him that I didn't seem to pick up on. Yet, I continued to have faith in him and the relationship. We spent many hours talking, and he opened up about some of his troubled past, which resulted in him leaving home by the time he was 16 years old. I sympathized with him and really believed in him. It seemed to me that many people misunderstood him. I felt like I understood him and wanted to be by his side helping him to be the better person I believed he could be. Gradually, I started to notice a few things that I now look back and recognize as red flags.

One day as we were walking in the woods by the school, he helped me over an old barricade of some sort, by hoisting me up over it. He made a passing comment about how good it would be if I actually started working out so I could tone my legs. It was very subtle, but it planted a seed of self-doubt about my body image—a thought that had previously never crossed my mind.

Later in the relationship, having introduced me to his family, he took me home for a family reunion. I was still getting to know everyone, and I'm by nature reserved in a new environment. I remember he took off with a friend for a while and I was left feeling a bit lost in the crowd. When he got back, I mentioned that I didn't like being left behind because he was the only one I really knew. Looking back at his reaction now, I realize that was a glimpse of how angry he could get. I don't remember everything he said, but I remember him reprimanding me and telling me not to embarrass him in front of his family. What I remember most vividly is one of his aunts observing his reaction and coming up to him. "I hope that's not how you talk to her," she said.

Since this was the first time I had seen him angry at me, I let it go and decided that I must have said something to upset him. I made a mental note to be sure not to upset him or embarrass him as he had asked. The first time I tried to break up with him, it was because I had begun to get uneasy about the direction of his life. He had got into enough trouble at this point to the extent of being suspended from school. I remember having a conversation with him letting him know I couldn't continue the relationship because he needed to figure out the direction he wanted to take in life. He pleaded with me to give him a chance. He asked me to wait for a while as he got his life in order. He soon enlisted in the military, and my heart softened, and I decided to give him a chance to prove himself. Very shortly after, he surprised me with an engagement ring that Christmas. This helped me to solidify my commitment to stand by him. He went off to basic training, and our relationship continued mostly by mail. We began to talk about marriage, and we agreed to get married earlier than originally planned so that we could take advantage of some of the military benefits including increased pay as a married soldier. During the next break he got out of training, we organized for a small, quick ceremony. I still wanted the wedding with all the glamor of being a bride, and he promised that with the increase in pay we could still have the wedding later in the year. We were happy with our decision and continued to live separately as he completed his training.

That summer, having completed his training, he came

to visit. I was still on campus as I worked at the school during breaks. Several events and conferences occurred on the campus during the school break, and I worked in various capacities during this time. During his visit, I remember having a conversation where we differed in opinion over a situation. He calmly stated, "You are my wife now, and you will do as I say." I think I actually laughed. I was sure he was joking. Then a chill ran down my spine as I realized he wasn't joking at all. That was the first time I thought to myself, "What have I done?"

CHAPTER TWO

Wedded Bliss

A few months after our small wedding ceremony, I found out I was expecting our first child. We were thrilled, yet a bit nervous because this was an early surprise. We, however, continued with our lives as he moved on into full military service. As planned, we went ahead and organized the wedding I had wanted. It was a sweet ceremony with close friends and family. We started our life together with hope and promise. We made the decision that I complete my last semester of school through distance learning from our new home. I spent a lot of time on my own because my husband worked long hours. Our home was about 20 or 30 minutes' drive from the military base. My husband would leave the house by 6 am and would be back about 7 pm. I kept busy with school work, but I always looked forward to spending time with him when he was home. With time, we started going through the usual irritations couples experience.

One particular evening we got into an argument. I don't remember what we disagreed over, but suddenly my husband struck me on the side of my face with his fist. I was so stunned. I had never imagined this could happen. I remember walking over to the closet and starting to get my clothes in an attempt to pack and get out of there somehow. I didn't have a plan; I just remember thinking to myself "I will never allow anyone to put his hands on me."

As I was methodically getting my clothes, I remember my husband by my side yelling in anger, asking what I was doing. I don't think I responded, I just calmly continued to pack. This really infuriated him. He grabbed hold of me and pinned me to the bed, telling me I wasn't going anywhere. This really terrified me, and for the first time, I realized he could really hurt me. I was about eight months pregnant at this point. I started to scream in fear, hoping our neighbors would hear me and come to my rescue. My screams seemed to calm my husband immediately, and he let go of me. I ran out of the house into the dark sobbing. I sat in the car for a while contemplating my next move. I could not believe what had just happened. As I sat there sobbing uncontrollably, my husband came out to me, visibly calm now. He began to soothe me and reassure me of his love. In the same breath, he calmly stated that I was being irrational and out of control, and it was his duty as my husband to control the situation. I was so confused. Was he right? Did I ask for it, and was it his duty to correct me? Was his method questionable? Or was this really just an incident where I pushed him far enough to make him hit me? That night, I fell asleep by his side with these thoughts plaguing my mind.

A month or so after that first major fight, life settled into an exciting rhythm as we welcomed our precious baby boy. We were excited, yet a bit nervous as we embraced our new role as parents. Life seemed normal, and the disturbing incident gradually settled at the back of my mind. As our baby grew, I started to think about getting some outside employment to supplement my husband's income, as well as give me something to do away from the mundane tasks in the home.

I started working a few hours a week for a daycare that allowed me to have my baby there with me. It worked well for a while, but gradually I realized it was not a good fit for me, so I started to look for something different. I found a position at a restaurant as a hostess. The atmosphere was great. However, the business was having some difficulty, and a few weeks after I was hired, the business closed down. I continued to search and decided to try the hotel industry. I applied to two places; one closer to our home at the time, and the other closer to the military base. I was pleasantly surprised to be accepted by both companies. I discussed the two opportunities with my husband to decide on which one I should accept. I told him one had slightly higher pay. His opinion stunned me. "You should accept the lower paying one. You've never done this before so why would you think you are qualified for the higher paying one?" I remember thinking to myself that as a college graduate surely, I had the capacity to learn, and should probably look for an even higher paying position. However, I didn't argue and accepted the lower paying job. I was unhappy with the training process and felt like I had to learn a lot on my own. Eventually, I told my husband this wasn't working out, and I wanted to try the other position if they would still have me. Fortunately, the position was still open, and I settled in well and even made friends with my colleagues who helped babysit our baby before my husband took over after work.

A year or so into the new job, my husband got orders to deploy out of the country. The area he was going to was not considered friendly so the military would not cover expenses for all of us to move. However, as a military wife with a husband on orders to deploy, I would receive special status and housing on the military base. I was excited at this prospect as I would be close to everything I needed regarding shopping, day care, and driving distance to work. I did not like to have to be separated that way, but I really thought our baby and I would be fine especially because I had made friends. My husband was completely against the idea and insisted I move to his parents' home. He said that he wanted the baby and I to be safe and protected. There wasn't much room for discussion, so we moved right before he was deployed.

I had a good relationship with my in-laws, so I settled in well, and I had the help I needed with the baby. They also enjoyed having their grandchild with them. I soon got a job at a nearby hotel and settled into a good rhythm.

Several months into the mission, my husband withdrew from the military. He came back home, and within weeks we lost all military benefits because of the nature of his untimely withdrawal. I remained supportive as he discussed with me his thoughts and his decision to withdraw. I had saved up enough in those months to rent our own place when he came home. I continued to work and support us as my husband struggled to find gainful employment. Gradually, he settled into a job and life was normal again.

Soon afterward, we started to have some significant issues that originated from my husband's habitual drinking as well as the abuse of narcotics. It spiraled into a full-fledged addiction, and soon we were having trouble paying bills. Although we were both gainfully employed, we both had access to the money, and he would withdraw large amounts to feed his habit.

As expected, we began to have a lot of tension and disagreements because of the financial stress. Things went from bad to worse. The drug and alcohol abuse got worse, and so did the arguments. Calm comes after the storm, the saying goes. This was true of our life. We would have peaceful, even joyous times until the next wave would hit. I remember an incident where my husband had taken off with our son and went to his friend's house. After multiple calls, I finally made my way to the home and found him drinking with his friends. I was upset and asked to take the child home. I don't remember whether he drove away from this place with our child or by himself. What I remember is that he almost ran me over with the car in anger.

On another occasion, I was furiously scrubbing the bathroom floor on my hands and knees in an attempt to get away from yet another argument. My husband followed me in a rage and dragged me up by my hair; I screamed in pain begging him to leave me alone. He soon calmed down and left me alone.

Another incident happened shortly after a blissful romantic getaway that my husband had set up. We had a great time as he went all out for me hiring a stretch limo, buying flowers and setting us up in a fancy hotel. Later that week, I took off in the middle of the night to stay with a friend I had made at a support group because my husband had angrily slapped and rained blows on me during an argument. I had to call off work the following morning.

As terrible as these incidences were, one particular night stands out. By this time, I had moved out several times but always came back to try to work things out. I had also looked for outside help and was working with a psychologist. I was considered clinically depressed and was on treatment.

I don't remember exactly what started an argument that night. I remember sitting on the bed trying to concentrate on a Bible study I was working on, so I could calm down and not fight anymore. I remember he followed me to the room and words were exchanged. Then it got physical. I remember being thrown against the wall, holding my hands over my head in a desperate effort to stop the blows that were being rained on me. When the storm passed, I lay there on the floor and thought to myself, "This is it. I am done. I cannot do this anymore." I had been to see my psychologist that week, and she had sent me to the doctor to get a new prescription for a higher dose of anti-depressants. I looked up from the floor, saw my two full bottles of the prescription pills on the dresser and didn't even think through the decision. I knew what I had to do. There were probably at least 20 small pills. With shaking hands, I opened the bottles and poured the pills into my hand. My husband, who had at that point walked away, came back to the room having calmed down. He had gone to get me a glass of iced tea. When he saw the pills in my hand, he asked what I was doing. He mocked me, handed me the glass and watched me swallow the pills in one gulp. Then instantly my mind cleared. I knew without a doubt that I was going to die. No one takes that amount of poison and walks away without help. I breathed a desperate prayer for help. I will forever remember the exact words I prayed. "Lord Jesus, if you will, please let me live."

Frantically, I started to look for my psychologist's number to call for help.

At that point, my husband stopped tormenting me with his words which included this phrase that is still etched in my memory "…and you better clean up this place before you (explicit word) die!" I think it dawned on him that I would indeed die. So, he got on the phone with his parents and asked them to come. I don't know what he said to them. I remember the shock on my father-in-law's face when he came and saw the war zone in our room with clothes and items strewn all over the floor. As he drove me to the hospital, he tried to engage me in a conversation to understand what was going on.

Before this incident, when the abuse had become more frequent, I had reached out to them and told them what was going on. His words to me at that time were, "I don't believe he hit you. I didn't raise him that way."

As that conversation played in my mind this time, I looked over at him and said, "You wouldn't believe me if I told you what happened."
When we got to the hospital, I was still walking, talking and thinking clearly.

I'll never forget the look on the receptionist's face when I placed the empty bottles on her desk and said, "I swallowed the contents of those two bottles and need help right now." In minutes I was in a room with tubes down my throat to pump out the contents of my stomach. As I lay on that table retching my guts out, I was fully aware of everything around me. The physician looked at me as he held the contents from my stomach that were now in a bucket. "Did you crush the pills?" he asked. "No, I did not." Orders were given to put another tube through my nose to try and neutralize the poison that was coursing through my bloodstream. The doctor said, "We need to try and get this stuff out before it makes your heart stop."

At some point, I stopped fighting, stopped struggling through the incredible pain and discomfort of having tubes down my nostrils. I could feel the poison working in my body. The doctor asked, "Does it feel better now?"

In a soft voice, as the fight left me, I said: "No, I feel worse." The doctor looked at me, shook his head and said, "Nothing, nobody, is worth dying like this for."

I wish I could say that after that incident, after I came out of that 48-hour period, that I gathered my things and left, never looking back. It would take another three years before I finally left for good. It would take being so scared that he'd actually finally kill me; after another episode of abuse, which at this time had become a refined art of not physically beating me but bullying me, threatening to burn my things, locking me up in the room to keep me from going anywhere. It was after I sat in a locked room, my cell phone taken away that I knew he would kill me one day. It took the help of friends to finally convince me to move in with them. It took the final desperate plea of my family for me to finally pick up one day, rent a car one-way, fill it up with only what could fit in it, leave my child behind with his grandparents and finally get the courage to choose life. Three years later, after that dark, dark night, I left the life I had known and drove into the unknown.

CHAPTER THREE

Breaking the Cycle

It is difficult to explain to anyone who has not been in an abusive situation why it is so hard to leave. For me, I always felt that perhaps there was one more thing I could do to fix it. I had taken my marriage vows seriously, and I really had a hard time justifying leaving. I also could not imagine leaving my son. But to effectively disconnect myself from that vicious cycle, that is exactly what I had to do. I left my son behind. You see, he had become a pawn in this game of control. I had effectively moved out of our home, but we still both had access to our son. I remember dropping him at school only to learn later that his dad made sure to get to the school before I did to pick him up. I had to get to the point where I was convinced that I could leave my son with his grandparents. It really wasn't a choice I thought I'd ever make, but I finally realized I couldn't live this life anymore. I knew deep within me that I'd die prematurely if I didn't change something. Moving out of the house to a place down the road was no longer effective. Not only did I leave my son behind, but I moved eight hours away from the home I had known. The distance was a crucial factor for me to begin my total healing process, and the ability to live a normal, healthy life. Getting to that point, however, was a journey.

The first time I looked for outside help, I walked into a mental health clinic. I was convinced that something was terribly wrong with me. The kind psychologist pointed out that I wasn't crazy, just really stressed and in need of some serious marital counseling. She referred me to a family counselor, to whom I will forever be grateful for giving me guidance that was the beginning of the end of the cycle. I learned that one of the biggest weapons that my husband could use against me was to isolate me from others. Getting an outside perspective may have been one of the best things I did for myself. Talking to someone with no particular opinion of me and my family or my circumstances offered a fresh perspective on my situation. My counselor introduced me to a support group which was a source of help for families of alcoholics or people with similar addictions. I learned some valuable lessons here. First of all, I found a group of people who just accepted me with all my problems because they got it. I could be myself and not worry about being judged because I wasn't the only one feeling so lost and confused. At the same time, there was structure, a channel for those feelings; there was order. There was also an opportunity for leadership as we took turns in leading meetings.

My counselor also introduced me to reading material. I like to read, so it was easy for me to read self-help books. I learned that the feelings I had were normal for the circumstances I was in.

Another thing that worked for me was finding a home church that allowed me to make new friends. This was my ticket to freedom. I found new acceptance and new perspectives and amazing love from people who took me in towards the end of the marriage. It is because of my friends that I finally found the courage to get up, walk out and start a fresh life.

The moment I finally gathered the courage to leave was after a lengthy conversation with my parents. They gently reassured me that my son would be fine if I left him in the care of his grandparents. They shared their fear for my life. That did it for me. I gathered my belongings, went to my in-laws and told them I was leaving, kissed my son goodbye, and drove eight hours away to live with my sister. When I actually moved across the country, I didn't have an option anymore to just go back home. The distance was a factor, and this was crucial for me to break the cycle and begin healing. I remember when I hit the six-month mark away, I realized that I had really done it this time. I had gradually regained control of my life.

Being away from the home situation, not having to deal with crises every waking moment helped my body, and mind to begin the healing process. I had learned to minimize the chaos and conflict. Communication with my husband was only by phone now, so when things started to escalate, I would just push the off button. I could control how much of the abuse I could tolerate. I didn't have to have that nasty voice in my ear calling me names.

I went back to school, worked a full-time job and gradually started getting involved in my new community. My sister was an integral part of this transition for me. Her gentle yet firm nature pushed me through periods of self-doubt and confusion. She helped to keep me grounded, busy, and in check.

The journey to healing was well underway.

CHAPTER FOUR

Moving On

I want to dedicate this chapter to that one person who will be reading this and wondering how to get out of the messy situation they find themselves in.

I'll start by acknowledging that I understand the feelings. Leaving an abusive home is tough. First of all, one has to acknowledge that this is indeed an abusive situation. I had to recognize that I was indeed in an abusive situation, that it was not a normal way of life, and I could choose not to live that way anymore. I encourage you to evaluate your situation, preferably with a trusted friend or better yet, a professional counselor. Looking for outside help was the key for me. I was able to see myself through someone else's eyes, and I began to realize how unhealthy my situation was.

I faithfully attended counseling sessions, which gave me the opportunity to think and talk through my situation. What counseling does is offer a safe place to think and come up with solutions. I didn't come to the conclusion to leave immediately. In fact, what I wanted was to have a peaceful and loving marriage. I told my husband about counseling, and he agreed to go with me. We attended the first session together; then our counselor had us come for individual sessions. It was during these individual sessions that my husband decided it was a waste of his time and did not follow through.

I tried other methods to help us as a couple. We attended a couple of church-based recovery programs that were recommended to us. We also had counseling from our pastor at the time. I really did try to do all that I knew to make things work. What I learned was that I only had control over how I changed and none over my husband's change. Granted, in a marriage, we can influence each other for better or for worse. As individuals, however, we can only control how we respond to counsel, and we can only decide for ourselves how to change.

As I was attending counseling, I also started to pursue further education. It was something I always wanted to do and so, through the guidance of some friends, I applied for school. It was important for me to pick the right kind of people to influence my life.

I also had a place I could go, far away from the home I knew. My sister lived several states away, and she invited me to live with her. It is important to have someone who loves you and that you completely trust, to help you with the transition. My sister did not give me a chance to sit in the house to wallow in my despair. After a few days of settling in, she pointed out several places within walking distance that I could go and apply for a job. She told me she would essentially need a progress report from my search. It wasn't long before I got a hotel job. Since I had been working in the industry for several years, I was able to get a position quickly. My sister also involved me in church activities and other community activities.

She did not really make room for me to say no. She would just tell me what she had planned and just expected me to go with her. This was very crucial for me, staying busy and involved helped me find new purpose and meaning to my life. You see, one of the reasons why anyone will stay in an abusive home is because somehow, we learn to manage. We learn to build walls of defense, armor for the battle, and survival techniques. It becomes the norm, and we don't know any other kind of life. In a way, what we know is more of a comfort zone than whatever may be out there. The fear of the unknown is very real.

My encouragement to anyone in this situation is to get out into the unknown. It takes a lot of strength and resilience to live through an abusive situation year after year. That same resilience will take one through the unknown. I didn't realize this until I took the leap. I have done better than just survive. I have, by God's grace, succeeded.

It is important to realize that as an individual in a similar situation as mine, your story will be different from mine. Depending on your situation, your network of support, your interests and perhaps various other factors, how you chose to leave your situation will be different. It is very important however to make an exit plan with help. It is difficult to think through a plan by yourself, so it is essential to find help.

Once you have decided on how to get out of the situation, understand that the healing process takes time. It may take a while to get over the feelings of fear, inadequacy, and confusion that you may feel. I am a big advocate for professional counseling because this helped me deal with those feelings in a healthy, effective way. Again, this took time. I was in counseling for years before I left my situation and went back to counseling thereafter.

On my own

My sister got married a year or so after I moved in with her. She and her husband were moving across the country, and she did not want to leave me behind. However, at this point in my life I had secured a job, enrolled in the local college, and I had begun to settle. I felt good enough to manage on my own. I had also made friends in the community. Reluctantly, she left me, after helping me secure my own apartment. With time, I was able to relocate my son from his father and grandparents to come live with me. I established a good network of friends who were invaluable to me. I was raising my son, going to work, and going to school. My son stayed at different friends' homes when I worked nights. Being a single parent is not an easy task. I struggled. Some days I literally would sit down and sob after a major explosion of emotions. It was at such times that I knew I needed to be very careful. I learned that I needed to look for that balance; to do whatever it takes to get rejuvenated again. My son struggled as well. He started acting up in school, requiring some minor disciplinary actions. I learned to look up to wise people around me to counsel me on parenting. Ultimately, I had to make the decisions that were right for my child and I, but it was good to have an outside perspective. I learned to take time out of my busy schedule to spend quality time with my son. I learned that this was crucial for his wellbeing. I taught him to reach out to me when he felt I had been too busy to spend time with him. I learned to take time out and even, when possible, take a weekend trip so we could be; just the two of us. What children really need is to feel secure in their parents' love and guidance. The rest falls into place so long as there is security and stability. I can proudly say I have a fairly well-adjusted teenager today.

One of the fears that an individual may experience when considering whether to leave an abusive situation or not is the impact on the children. I believe that children suffer more in an abusive environment. They adjust better in a stable, secure environment even when there are hiccups along the way. One of the wise statements that my counselor said to me back when I was contemplating leaving my situation was this; as long as I was alright, my son would be too.

I have found this to be true. We have gone through several adjustments along the way, but so long as I'm a source of stability and love to him, he thrives.

Another fear that one may experience is the fear of being alone. I found that once I moved out of my home, I seemed to reminisce more on the good times in our marriage, and I really missed that companionship. One of the factors that played a major role in helping me slowly move on was the distance. It is crucial to create physical and emotional distance in order to heal.

I feel like I stumbled through singlehood. I went through a lot of trial and error. However, I don't regret the lessons I learned along the way. I learned the kind of boundaries I needed for healthy relationships. My counselor said something to me during one of our sessions. She said she feared that I might make another mistake with a relationship because I had learned to deal with so much pain. She was afraid I would settle for someone who would perhaps not be abusive but would take advantage of me somehow, and I would be alright with it. She hoped I would learn to have healthy relationships. I must confess that this was the greatest challenge for me. Along the way, I began to wonder if I would ever get this area of my life right. With each potential long term relationship, I learned more about myself and more about the kind of partner I desired. Time was a crucial factor in my growth and healing process. It took me literally years to be ready for a good, healthy, long term relationship. Today my life is transformed. I have a stable career, recently married to the most wonderful man, and we have adjusted well to this life. The resilience I developed while in my tough home situation helped me through. I look back and marvel at how far I have come in a few years. I certainly give all the glory to God for I attribute my transformation to Him.

CHAPTER FIVE

Help through the journey

Back when I was going through that difficult season of my life, I found it tough to share with friends and family what was really going on. On occasions when I did gather the courage to tell someone, I would get some very interesting responses that were not very helpful.

"I would fight back. Why don't you fight him back?"

"All couples struggle, you just need to ask the Lord to help you."

"You need to calmly work things out and talk through

them." These are just some of the responses I got from friends, family, clergy and even the police force.

I hope in this chapter I can help those who are on the outside apply effective ways to communicate with someone in an abusive situation. Let me use the above statements to clarify why those responses are not effective.

In my case, my husband was a taller, stronger, trained military man. I would be foolish to try and fight him back. Now granted, I did try a couple of times to defend myself, but he would very quickly overpower me. He was also able to really control himself without exerting all his strength. Abuse is a power issue. It is also not always physical. In fact, a good portion of it was emotional abuse.

The second statement, to me, almost seems to excuse abuse. Abuse is not a typical everyday struggle for most couples. It is a serious issue that deserves serious consideration and intervention. I want to illustrate how minimizing domestic abuse to everyday marital struggles can be a terrible oversight that could have devastating consequences.

One Sunday morning, my husband was in a rage

following a disagreement that occurred the previous evening. He locked me in a room after threatening to burn my things, took my cell phone away and essentially kept me from going to church. He finally calmed down enough to have me drive us to church. After the service, I quickly went to the pastor and elders to let them know that I didn't feel safe going back home. They summoned my husband to talk to him while I waited outside. I talked to my friend who stayed behind with me. When I shared my fears with her, she asked if she could take our son home with her. She wanted to take me along as well, but I wanted to know how the meeting would turn out and what intervention would be made. To my disbelief, I was sent back home with my husband as he had told the elders that I was always free to come and go as I chose and there was not a reason for me to be afraid.

On the way home, I had to endure my husband's anger as he spat out words of contempt for telling the men of the church one of whom, at the time, was unmarried. "He doesn't even understand what it takes to deal with a wife, what does he think he can say to me?" As I took the driver's seat at the request of my husband who was at the time on a suspended driver's license, he demanded that I tell him where our son was, and what I was planning to do. I told him our son was with friends. He demanded I drive to our friend's house, but I told him that I did not think that was a good idea. This infuriated him and, in an effort to literally take control of the wheel, he reached out to the gear, changed it to neutral as he reached for the steering wheel. Although I was in the driver's seat, my husband brought the car to a stop in the middle of the road from the passenger's seat. I was terrified. I ran out of the car in the middle of the road, flagged down oncoming traffic and pleaded for someone to help me. The motorists called the police, and within moments we were surrounded. My husband took off before the police got there.

I remember recognizing one officer. He had responded to my call during an earlier incident when I felt threatened at home. This particular officer had come home to find a very calm, polite man washing dishes, while his frantic wife described how terrified she was of him. He left that day after reprimanding me and asking me to just work things out politely with my husband.

As my eyes locked with his as he responded to the incident at hand, I greeted him with a nervous laugh and an "I told you so" look.

I don't entirely blame my dear church members or the hardworking police force for the way they responded. One has to understand what you are dealing with in order to deal with it effectively.

My suggestion would be that friends, family, clergy and police force should always err on the side of caution. Always choose to believe the alleged victim. By the time they come for help, they are truly in grave danger. Get them to a safe place first, then investigate. Never deliver them back to the hands of the alleged aggressor. You may actually be handing them over to their death.

In the case where a victim may not come for help, but you suspect there is abuse going on, be cautious in how you approach the subject, but approach it. Be someone that is genuinely interested and compassionate and willing to listen and support for the long haul. Also, a victim may not readily accept help if you are the one suggesting it. Be available for when she is ready to get help and know that it may take a while.

Don't scold her or point out the aggressor's weaknesses. Remember this is a person she loves and will stand by him first and foremost.

My best friend is a great example of the kind of friend who sticks through to the end. She literally called me every day, twice a day for months until I finally left and moved to a safe place several states away. She would listen to me and always let me know she was ready to help in whatever way. She may not have been able to rescue me physically, but she stayed in touch often enough to be able to detect danger and would have been able to mobilize help if she was ever required to do so. Be a great friend and confidant.

To the clergy, I would humbly appeal that sensitivity is vital. Avoid lumping an abusive situation in the same category as other common marital problems. In fact, I would go a step further and encourage members of the clergy to research on domestic abuse. There are several great resources. Be teachable and recognize how prevalent this phenomenon is in our communities today. Be willing to find practical ways to deal with it rather than over-spiritualizing the issue.

Humbly seek answers from professionals equipped to handle this situation. An even better way to deal with this would be to get educated in this area so that you can be the professional to deal with this from a perspective that is in line with your church leadership.

Let us all do our part. Let us no longer shy away and bury our heads in the sand. Domestic abuse is alive and well, and it kills. Let us do our part to minimize this prevalent phenomenon in our communities, and help those among us living this painful reality in their homes.

HELPFUL RESOURCES

The National Domestic Violence Hotline

1-800-799-SAFE (7233)

Citizens Against Spousal Abuse (CASA)- Look in your local listings for a local chapter. They offer legal counsel, shelter, among other resources.

Young Women's Christian Association (YWCA)- Look in your local listings for a local chapter. They offer educational programs, counseling, and other resources.

1. http://ncadv.org/learn-more/what-is-domestic-violence

Praise For
Battered, Broken, Healed

In a poignant account of courage through years of intimate partner violence, Miriam allows us to experience the dark and raw moments of this hurtful experience, and the eventual celebration of a valiant and victorious breakthrough. This book inspires courage and breathes a message of hope to survivors of domestic violence and their loved ones.

- **Mercy Mwaria-Mpolokoso**

The story line in this book reads like fiction, but yet domestic abuse is real and happening to far too many women and men. I applaud the author, Miriam, for sharing her story candidly for the sake of others and shedding light on a dark subject that often gets shoved to the corner.

- **Catherine Gathuka Franklin**

If this book does nothing else, let it highlight that "abuse is not a typical everyday struggle for most couples. It is a serious issue that deserves serious consideration and intervention."

Miriam writes about how she almost got so inured to the domestic abuse she underwent, that she nearly developed a pattern of seeking out abusive relationships to replace the one she managed to walk out of. But the key takeaway from this invaluable book is that she not only walked out of an abusive marriage but that she also found a wholesome one years later. This book is above all a key testament to the unbreakable human spirit that each one of us can have access to. If you are the victim of abuse, do not give up. Do not accept your "fate." a better life awaits you.

- **James Gachau**

CPSIA information can be obtained
at www.ICGtesting.com
Printed in the USA
LVOW13s0000280617
539620LV00009B/97/P